C000125265

Albert
19 Ynyswen Sirnowy view
Pontllanfraith
Blackwood, South Wales
UK   NP12 2GW

Published in the U.K. by
Old Bakehouse Publications
Church Street,
Abertillery, Gwent NP13 1EA
Telephone: 01495 212600 Fax: 01495 216222

Website: www.oldbakehouseprint.co.uk

Made and printed in the UK
by J.R. Davies (Printers) Ltd.

British Library Cataloguing in Publication Data: a catalogue
record for this book is available from the British Library.

Foreword

HOUSE OF COMMONS
LONDON SW1A 0AA

Brian Collins and Terry Powell have produced a little gem in their latest volume of *Crumlin to Pontymister – Then & Now*.

When I worked as a journalist before becoming MP for Islwyn, we used to say a picture is worth a thousand words.

Our authors have certainly proved the point.

They have captured in pictures the very dramatic changes in the landscape of our valleys these past years.

With the passing of heavy industry, the valleys are green again and who could have said 20 years ago the mining valleys of Gwent would become a tourist attraction?

I think it is so important we record our heritage both in pictures and words. History books are full of the legends of kings, queens, and great events.

Yet all too few record the history of valley communities in the way *Then & Now* manages to do. We have a rich and proud history and Brian and Terry have succeeded in bringing it to life.

Typically, the profits from the sale of this book will go to Tŷ Hafan Children's Hospice. That in itself speaks volumes about the sort of people who live in the valleys and whose time, past and present, is recorded in this book.

Don Touhig MP
Member of Parliament for Islwyn
Under Secretary of State for Wales
28 July 2003

Contents

Introduction

In collecting photographs for their earlier publications, *Old Crumlin to Pontymister in Photographs, Volumes 1 and 2,* the authors were often struck by the changes which have taken place in this section of the valley. This has led to the intense photographing of current views to provide the visual comparisons set out in this book. Wherever possible, the new pictures have been obtained by seeking out the original camera positions, and retaining scale and orientation. In some cases, kind property owners have permitted access to their driveways, fields, and even upstairs windows! An attempt has been made to give a complete coverage of the part of the valley in question, but restrictions have been imposed through the availability of old photographs of the desired quality and content.

A very noticeable change present in so many of the examples shown is the recent extensive growth of vegetation. This of course has caused problems in finding the appropriate camera positions, which will account for some misalignments. One of the reasons for this rapid growth of trees is likely to be the run-down of heavy industries - coal mining, steel, by-products, etc., and their replacement with light manufacturing. Again, as so many of the photographs show, chimneys have disappeared from dwelling houses as coal fires have been replaced by cleaner gas or electrical heating systems.

Global warming is also a factor to be considered. These changes have brought about a transformation in the appearance of the hillsides. The resulting colourful scenery could well lead to a film sequel entitled HOW GREEN *IS* MY VALLEY!

The older pictures display the family-type communities which existed in past times. With the slow horse and trap travel, combined with shanks's pony, people in the villages had regular contact with one another. This lessened with the development of regular bus and train services, and has become almost nonexistent today with the ownership of private cars, and of multi-media entertainment systems at home. A certain amount of community spirit still exists however, particularly when compared to larger towns and cities.

For the technically minded, the current photographs were taken using an Olympus Camedia 5050 digital camera, producing 5 million pixels. The images were obtained directly in greyscale, needing very little computer manipulation thereafter.

As the project is essentially visual, it becomes necessary to publish the photographs as large as possible. This means that the descriptive captions have been restricted in length. The reader will therefore find many changes to add to those mentioned.

It is hoped that the illustrations will bring back many pleasant memories. They are sure to raise many questions as to *'where?', 'when?'* and perhaps even *'why?'*

Brian Collins   Terry Powell.

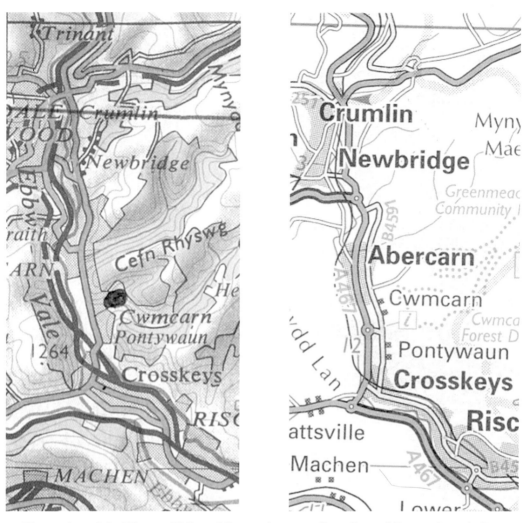

The section of the Western Valley of Gwent, between Crumlin and Pontymister, before and after the construction of the A467 bypass road.

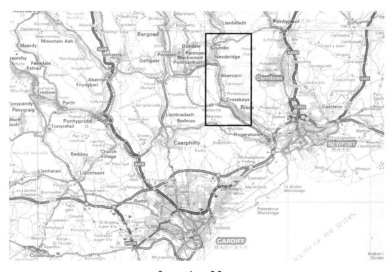

Location Map

Chapter 1

Crumlin

1. In 1900, temperance was the order of the day at Crumlin. At the foot of Hillside, the Cyclist's Rest and the Temperance Hotel opposite, encouraged compliance.

2. A new bypass road now separates Hillside from the square, which is dominated by the Navigation Workmen's Institute - now used as a County Community Education Centre. The Temperance Hotel was replaced by The Empire, first a theatre and later a cinema, which in turn has given way to the Crumlin Old Age Pensioners' Hall.

3. Crumlin Square c.1900. A farm overlooked the level crossing on the main Newport to Ebbw Vale railway line, whilst a small bridge was sufficient to clear the river and canal. The hillside opposite was quite empty, and on the right was one of the many Temperance Hotels which Lady Llanover was instrumental in bringing to the valley.

4. Lewis Street can now be seen on the skyline. The edge of The Railway Hotel protrudes beyond the Institute building. The height of the road, raised to clear the railway, can be gauged from the windows of The Viaduct Hotel, the long white building in the centre of the picture. The brick-built pharmacy in the centre of the square, replaced the chemist's shop which was demolished by a runaway lorry in the 1990s.

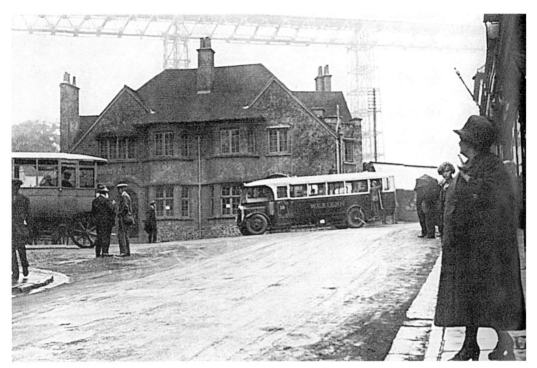

5. Crumlin Square was a busy place in the 1920s, overshadowed by the viaduct, which was constructed in 1857 by T.W. Kennard at a cost of £62,000. The Railway Hotel was built at the same time. The road to Ebbw Vale and Pontypool bears off to the right, towards the *'new'* bridge over the railway.

6. The viaduct was demolished in 1966. The road to the right has been closed to traffic, whilst The Railway Hotel shows the benefit of the cleaner atmosphere.

7. A Lewis & James bus on its way along Main Street towards Newbridge during the 1930s. A flourishing shopping centre existed at that time.

8. The shops on the left-hand side have changed little but the houses above Crown Street have vanished. The entire block on the right has been demolished to make way for the Old Age Pensioners' Hall. Beneath the hall can be seen a beautiful wall mosaic illustrating the village's history.

9. Crumlin Square in the 1950s, looking relatively peaceful - even though it was still on the main road up the valley. Griff's Tailoring Service was still going strong on the left.

10. The square is now a quiet cul-de-sac, but still with a good range of shops. The new mosaic beneath the Old Age Pensioners' Club is the only reminder of the past.

11. Looking along Main Street, Crumlin c.1900, the road dipped dramatically beyond the village square towards the low-level crossing. The Viaduct Tavern was just one of many public houses in the town.

12. A hundred years later and the raising of the road is evident, originally for access to a succession of bridges built over the railway line and river. Now the road terminates in the cul-de-sac of the square. Mr. Lewis's establishment is now the Crumlin Ex-Servicemen's Club.

13. Further back along Main Street was the New Inn.

14. Today's view, photographed from the bottom of Mining School Hill. The town centre is bypassed, the through road meeting the B4251, with options of left to Oakdale or right to the A467. Where the New Inn once stood is now a much more modern building, The Patriot. Several properties further along have been demolished.

15. The viaduct dominated a rather muddy Crown Street in the 1900s. On the left, near the large telegraph pole, can be seen the Police Station and the Mynyddislwyn Board School which opened in 1885 and closed in 1930.

16. No longer a through road, and with the major addition of the large brick building on the left. Opened as the Woodbine Club in 1925, it is now a sports outfitter's warehouse.

17. Crumlin Hall, built by T.W. Kennard for his own use whilst building the viaduct, became the venue for many musical evenings. Crumlin College opened in 1914, and in 1930 it became Monmouthshire Mining and Technical College. The name was changed again in 1948 to Technical College of Monmouthshire, Crumlin.

18. The house was demolished in the early 1960s, but the site continues its educational connections as the Crumlin Annexe to Coleg Gwent. The majority of the courses have been transferred to Crosskeys.

19. Commercial Road, off Hillside, lived up to its name until that fateful night in 1915. The fire started in Brammer's outfitter's shop, and quickly spread through all four. The estimated damage was £2,000!

20. Renovated as dwelling houses - an excellent match with the rest of the terrace. What would the work cost today?

21. Navigation Colliery, began full production in 1911, alongside the older Budd's Colliery. Sinking began in 1907 by Partridge Jones & Company. It was a model pit in its time, its surface buildings resplendent with yellow and red brickwork.

22. Production ceased in 1968, and some of the colliery buildings have found other uses, including the sale of second-hand car spares and furniture upholstery. The railway sidings have made way for the A467 bypass road.

23. An idyllic view from the 1900s. D.F. Pritchard's Brewery can be seen under the viaduct, with the Newport - Crumlin canal ending at the turning pool just beyond the canal bridge. The large stone-built building in the foreground was the Dodd's Building built by the family who, as cider purveyors and later gas installers and suppliers, contributed much to the development of Crumlin from the 1870s.

24. The A467 bypass road changes it all, and the demolition of the Dodd's Building allows the whole of The Old Navigation Hotel to be seen. The long white building visible in both pictures is The Viaduct Hotel.

25. By the 1930s, the low-level railway crossing had been replaced by a bridge spanning the main line from Newport to Ebbw Vale. The impressive building, front left, was the Palace (known as *'White Elephant'*) Theatre, which was also the venue for many boxing contests. The Workmen's Institute, and the Empire complex opposite, dominated the village square.

26. Some 50 years later, the A467 bypass road, in the foreground, removed most of the traffic from the village centre. Then, in the 1990s, the new railway/river bridge to the right opened up the route to Croespenmaen, closing the square to through traffic. Many of the early landmarks are gone.

27. A full load of coal trucks crossing the viaduct, and needing two engines to handle it. Pritchard's Western Valley Brewery is the dark-roofed building to the left, housed in what was originally Kennard's Viaduct Workshop. The Railway Hotel can be seen through the centre span of the bridge.

28. The valley looks much wider without the viaduct. One has to look hard to locate The Railway Hotel between the two bridges. Much more housing is evident on the hillside above the village, and new factories occupy the brewery site. The remains of the stone abutment of the viaduct can be seen in the hillside on the extreme left.

Chapter 2

Newbridge

29. Looking towards Cwmdows from High Street, there were empty fields on the skyline behind Twyn Gwyn Terrace. Up until the end of the nineteenth century, Cwm Dws, as it was then called, was an isolated group of five or six homesteads quite separate from Newbridge.

30. The roofs of the bungalows on the Homeleigh Estate can just be seen behind Twyn Gwyn. The derelict ground has become Windsor Avenue park, adding greatly to the attractiveness of the scene. Several other buildings can also be identified in both pictures.

31. Celynen Collieries Workmen's Institute was built and maintained by the weekly contributions from the miners in the local collieries. It housed a billiards hall, library, reading room and various meeting rooms.

32. Towering above the original Institute building is the Memorial Hall cinema and dance hall. The whole complex is now called Newbridge Institute and plans are in hand for its future preservation and use. Just visible on the left is the new Police Station.

33. Y Deml, the church seen in the background of this picture, was inaugurated in 1891, and was replaced by the Temple Calvinistic Methodist Church. Here we see the laying of the foundation stone of the latter in 1912, its opening being in February 1913.

34. The site of the Temple Church is now occupied by the new Police Station and a small car park. The rear of Meredith Terrace can be identified in both pictures.

35. The arrival of the photographer raised a lot of interest outside Newbridge Hotel. The building seen behind the horse and cart was erected in 1893, and the shop was later to provide sweets to the many on their way to the cinema.

36. The open spaces to the right of the road have been built upon and the large building, now a betting office, has been extended outwards on the ground floor level.

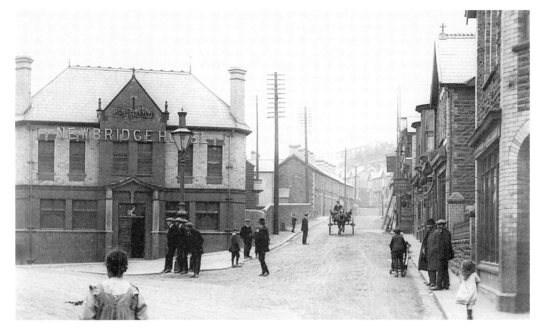

37. The buildings at the lower end of Tynewydd Terrace, which date from 1893, showed a wide variety of design. They provided a mixture of shops and houses, including well-known proprietors, such as Marsh (greengrocery) and Target (electrical services).

38. Much more uniformity in the shop frontages is evident nowadays, whilst the exterior of the hotel has changed little. Its name however, has changed to The Newbridge.

39. The Trecelyn Stores looked out on a quiet lower end of High Street before the Tabernacle Baptist Chapel was re-built.

40. Still looking very quiet, but the stores being much grander as a major bank, having housed two other banks in the meantime. The buildings to the right have now all been converted into commercial use. The imposing roof of the Tabernacle Baptist Chapel, re-built in 1912, can now be seen to the left of centre.

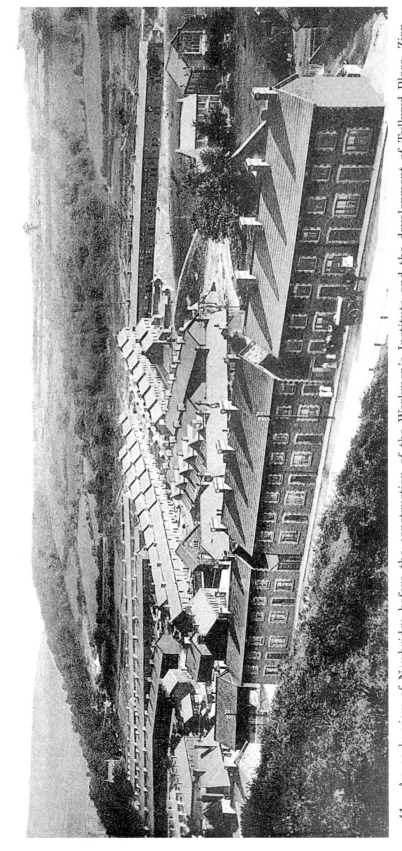

41. An early view of Newbridge before the construction of the Workmen's Institute and the development of Tyllwyd Place. Zion Congregationalist Church, dating from 1897, then looked out on to an empty field. The roof of Tynewydd Primary School can just be seen in the lower right-hand corner. The picture was taken a few years before Y Deml church was replaced by Temple, (see photograph 33).

42. The empty field is now occupied by St Paul's Church, built in the 1920s. Behind that can be seen the Memorial Hall cinema, which opened in 1924. The houses in front of the church are part of Cwrt Tynewydd, built on the site of the school which was demolished in 2000. Zion has now become a United Reformed Church. Above the rooftops on the extreme left is Trecelyn Viaduct, being part of the new bypass road.

43. Jones & Porter Ltd., who had stores throughout the valley, opened their warehouse in Station Square in 1932. The large building to the right was Frazer's vegetable warehouse and the sign directing travellers to the GWR station can be partly seen on the right. In the distance, the Lucania Billiard Hall boasted 6 tables.

44. The billiard hall became Newbridge Labour Club, with the station and much of the square being turned into a car park. Connections with the grocery trade have been maintained by the warehouse becoming a supermarket.

45. The view above the subway in Newbridge. On the left was the old Police Station, built in 1902, and several shops can be seen in the complex which was later to house the billiards hall.

46. The whole of the building in the centre now makes up the Labour Club.

47. The view from Newbridge Station, c.1930. Blaen Bloddau Farm was the large white building in front of Beynon Street. Note the sidings on both sides of the main line where coal trucks could await their turn to move.

48. The railway line was closed in 1962 to all traffic other than freight to and from Ebbw Vale Steelworks, which in turn closed in 2002. There are plans to re-open the line for passenger trains again in 2005. The farm too has disappeared.

49. A view towards Crumlin from the old tram road, c.1900. Celynen North Colliery was still to be built, and Treowen Housing Estate did not appear until the 1920s. Newbridge Town Hall, later to become the Grand Cinema, was the large building centre right.

50. Much new building in evidence, including the white tower of Our Lady of Peace Catholic Church in the centre of the picture. Beyond the school and leisure centre buildings to the right, Celynen North Colliery has come and gone - partly replaced by the giant electronics factory of Aiwa Wales Manufacturing.

51. Looking towards Pantside from above Beynon Street, the grammar school, opened in 1926, dominated the picture. On the hill, the large house Llwyncelyn was in splendid isolation, whilst Pant Farm and its outbuildings could be seen in the clearing to the right. The Welfare Ground lay in the right foreground.

52. Many extensions to the school buildings have appeared as has the Pantside Housing Estate, built in the mid 1950s. The long white building on the left is the Aiwa electronics factory, built on the site of Celynen North Colliery.

53. Newbridge Wesley Hall on Bridge Street.

54. Newbridge Methodist Church was built on the open space in front of Wesley Hall in 1952. Two views of the church are shown in order to illustrate that the Hall was not demolished but is now used as a workshop for a local joinery business, seen behind and to the right. The schoolroom, referred to as the Lesser Hall, was obtained in the early 1920s from North Wales, where it had been used as a wartime hospital hut. In the mid 1940s, it improvised as an overspill classroom for the nearby Grammar School. It is again seen behind, but to the left of the Methodist Church.

55. A view of Newbridge Boxing Club towards the end of its life. Made famous in recent times by World Champion Joe Calzaghe, the building was erected by the Miners' Welfare in the 1920s, and housed changing rooms for Newbridge Rugby Football Club.

56. The space left by its demolition in 2002 looks ripe for re-development. Newbridge Rugby Clubhouse in the background was originally the Boys' Club.

57. The main Newport road crossed the canal on its way to Newbridge and Crumlin, the narrow road on the right leading only to Pantside. The lock-keeper's cottage could just be made out amongst the trees - beside the lock on the far side of the bridge.

58. Almost exactly on the site of the old bridge is a new roundabout, with major by-pass roads leading to Maesycwmmer in the one direction, and to Crumlin in the other.

59. Pant Farm, being over 300 years old, stands at the bottom of the small valley leading to Coed Cillonydd.

60. The farm exists now as The Stables B & B, and is mostly hidden behind the trees on the left. Much of its land has been used to build Central Avenue, gateway to the Pant Housing Estate. The main road at the bottom of the picture is the by-pass road to Crumlin, built over the canal.

61. Looking down Central Avenue, Pantside, Pant Farm is hidden behind the trees lower down on the right.

62. An addition to the scene is the Trecelyn Viaduct, part of the new road which leads directly to Maesycwmmer, skirting Newbridge, Pentwynmawr, and Pontllanfraith en route.

63. Celynen South Colliery days after closure in 1985. Sinking began in 1873, and coal production commenced in 1876. It began under the ownership of the Newport-Abercarn Black Vein Steam Coal Company, and finished up belonging to the National Coal Board. It was one of the last mines to raise coal using a steam powered winding engine.

64. The site is now in the early stages of development for mixed dwellings - an estimated 400 properties. Plans include other facilities - such as shops etc. A great deal of earth moving and ground stabilisation is necessary before any building work can commence.

Chapter 3

Abercarn

65. An idyllic canal scene at Chapel of Ease. High Meadow housing estate, built in the early 1950s, commanded the hillside ahead.

66. From this point southwards, as far as Crosskeys, the canal has been replaced by the A467 bypass road, but it still exists northwards as far as Newbridge. The temporary fencing seen on the left will soon give way to an access to the housing development taking place on the site of the old Celynen South Colliery.

67. This picture of Abercarn is easy to date, as the house under construction on Pantyresk Road, on the distant hillside, was completed in 1901. Abercarn Colliery's No.1 Pit lay in the immediate foreground, and Victoria Hall cinema to the front left.

68. Much more development at Pantyresk. Several noticeable absentees include the four rows of The Ranks, Victoria Hall and the Garn Congregational Church, built in the mid 1840s.

69. St. Luke's Church, Abercarn, standing atop the quarry once worked by Robert Evans & Company. The bridge in the foreground still passes from the West End, over the railway, and down to Chapel of Ease.

70. The church building, unused for some time, has fallen into a poor state of repair. The space created by the quarry is now used as a haulage depot and for warehousing. The immediate tinworks structures have disappeared, and the line of the canal is taken up by the A467 bypass road. These pictures really serve to emphasise how vegetation has flourished in recent years.

71. High Street, Abercarn, c.1900, when it was a thriving commercial part of the village. Several more shops and houses were to be found on the right, around the bend in the road. The Garn Congregational Church stood proud on the left.

72. The most striking difference here is the absence of all the older buildings on the right-hand side. In fact, if they still existed, they would be standing on the realigned road - parts of their back walls are still seen in the bank. The old road forms a lay-by in front of the remaining structures on the left. The Post Office is followed by a row which has been hardly altered. The site where the Garn Chapel stood is now being built upon, and the terrace blocks up to the turn in the road are still intact.

73. The Council Offices, Abercarn, pictured before the cenotaph was constructed in 1924 - a field gun serving as a temporary memorial. This was the site of a market place, opened in 1846, above which was a room known as Market Hall used for public meetings, religious services, concerts, and lectures.

74. Abercarn Urban District Council was replaced by Islwyn Borough Council in 1974. The Council Offices were demolished in 1979 and Gwyddon Court built in their place. St. Luke's Surgery is now seen on the left.

75. A view obtained in the early 1980s, from an elevated camera position, shows the Council Offices surrounded by several interesting features.

To the left was Abercarn Miners' Institute, opened in 1925 and replaced in 1994 by St. Luke's Surgery. The surgery was located for several years in part of the Institute building, having moved from its earlier address in Commercial Road.

In the foreground are the remaining sections of The Ranks, which were themselves removed in 1983. The original four rows were built by Ebenezer Rogers, and were once described as creating a *'Model Village'*. A complex of modern flats now stands on the site.

On the hillside, amongst the trees can be seen Lady Llanover's Welsh Presbyterian Church, which still conducts services in the Welsh language. Church in Wales services are also held in the Welsh Church, St Luke's Church building becoming disused.

Gwyddon School, to the right, has seen many changes, and is now a Welsh medium school, Ysgol Gymraeg Cwm Gwyddon.

These strong influences follow long after the setting up of a Welsh Movement under the patronage of Sir Benjamin and Lady Hall - Sir Benjamin's name is preserved for posterity through his connection with the bell in the clock tower at Westminster.

The Rechabites Hall, just along Gwyddon Road from the old Institute still exists, and is used for services by the Garn United Reform Church.

Abercarn is one of the villages in the valley that has suffered commercially as a result of the building of the bypass road, with the loss of shops and other facilities.

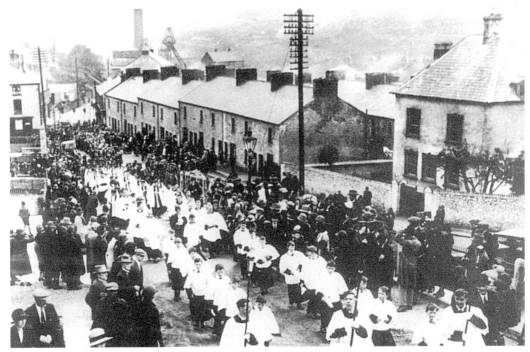

76. A Church parade making its way from the old tin church in the West End in Abercarn to St Luke's, soon after its opening in 1928. The tin church itself was built in 1890. The Tinplate Manager's house is seen on the immediate right, with The Ranks further along. The headgear of Prince of Wales Colliery provided the backdrop.

77. The main visual change here is the replacement of the old Ranks terraces with modern blocks of flats - also named The Ranks. The Tinplaters' Institute, which was just out of shot on the right, has now become the clubhouse of Abercarn Rugby Football Club.

78. The Abercarn branch of these well known outfitters commanded a prime position on the corner of High Street and Bridge Street.

79. The premises have seen several businesses over the years, but their eventual fate has been conversion into flats. This part of Bridge Street has now become a cul-de-sac having been cut off by the A467 bypass road. The roof of a factory in the Prince of Wales Industrial Estate is seen straight ahead.

80. The Church Lads' Brigade, proudly marching through Abercarn. The entrance stairway to Victoria Hall is seen alongside. The Hall was opened in 1902 as a concert hall, and was later used as a cinema. It closed in 1945 and was demolished in 1971. In the immediate background was the Salvation Army Hall, later used as a garage and filling station, and further back the headgear of Prince of Wales Colliery.

81. What a clearance! A much more open aspect with the area taken up by a car sales business. The picture at least offers a clear view of Cilfynydd Farm on the hillside above Cwmcarn.

82. A picturesque image of the canal bridge at Abercarn, gaining access to the Prince of Wales Colliery site. The colliery lamproom was to the left of the canal bank, whilst Victoria Hall could be seen alongside the main road to the right.

83. The canal has been completely replaced by the A467 bypass road. The turn off to the left leads to the West End and to the Prince of Wales Industrial Estate. The old colliery lamproom can again be seen on the left. It now houses a furniture business.

84. A very unhealthy image of Abercarn around 1947, with the New Tinworks, opened in 1911, pouring out most of the pollution. The earlier iron industry in the area dates back to the 16th century, being attributed to Richard Hanbury.

85. The tinworks building now houses a trolley refurbishment company, and forms part of the Abercarn Industrial Estate - several other undertakings are masked by the trees. Vegetation seems to have thrived in the cleaner air.

86. West End, Abercarn, c.1905. The old iron foundry could just be seen over the trees, with a fair mix of other industrial operations in evidence. The gasworks was transferred to the other side of the river in the early 1950s, and was recently removed completely.

87. Many of the streets still exist, the appearance of the whole area profiting from an EU funded improvement scheme. The housing developments of High Meadow and Persondy are in evidence on the far hillside, together with extensive quarrying operations at the top of the valley above Chapel of Ease.

88. Bridge Street, Abercarn, c.1920, with the tinworks on the left.

89. Very little alteration to the buildings on the right, apart from some changes in use. The structure that housed the New Tinworks can be seen on the left, whilst hidden behind the trees are the Royal Mail Delivery Office, and the Abercarn Industrial Estate.

90. The lower end of Islwyn Street, Abercarn, around 1910. Plenty of commercial activity and interest in the photographer.

91. All but two shops (the Post Office and a minimarket) have disappeared. Some demolition on the left has made way for the West End road towards Newbridge. The old tinworks building provides an imposing background.

92. Islwyn Street in Abercarn's West End, c.1905. The entrance at the front left led to the Vicarage.

93. Little change apart from the inevitable addition of telephone lines, and electrical services. The Vicarage was replaced in 1938 by the development of Troedyrhiw.

94. Prince of Wales Colliery, Abercarn, sunk in 1865 by the Ebbw Vale Company. Its place in history will be marked by the disaster of 11th September 1878, when an explosion caused the deaths of 264 men and boys. The white building on the extreme left was the lamproom, and is one of the few remaining structures from the colliery. It was used as a temporary mortuary at the time of the explosion.

95. The old lamproom is now used by a furniture company, and is part of the Prince of Wales Industrial Estate, which was established in 1970. Many more houses have been built on Rhyswg Road, seen on the hill in the background.

96. The view northwards along Commercial Road in Abercarn, as it appeared in the late 1940s. The elevated terrace on the right is Darren View, and the bridge over the canal to the left led to Prince of Wales Colliery and to Abercarn Welfare Ground.

97. Rapid increase in the ownership of private motor vehicles, together with the establishment of the National Coal Board's No.6 Area Headquarters, just off to the left, created an urgent need for road widening at this location. The view above is from the early 1950s.

98. A further major change in the road layout, the canal being completely covered by the new A467 bypass. This section was opened in 1969, the old road being re-named as B4591. The formation level of the roads was substantially raised, as can be seen from the much lower height of the retaining wall in front of Darren View.

Prince of Wales Colliery had remained open for many years for pumping, and as a safety connection to Cwmcarn Colliery. Just a few small buildings now remain from the colliery, the remainder of the site, behind the trees on the left, being given over to the Prince of Wales Industrial Estate, which was opened by the then Prime Minister, Mr. Harold Wilson, in 1970.

Buildings seen in the centre of the two earlier photographs were the Social Centre, and, behind, the Central Hall. The aptly named Social Centre was a widely used facility for a variety of purposes, its function nowadays taken over by the Scout Hut.

The Social Centre was removed for the construction of the bypass, whose route, however, ran alongside the Central Hall, a chapel found suitable for holding concerts and other more formal events, and itself being demolished in the late 1990s.

Apart from the improvement in the roads, the photographs also serve to highlight how street lighting has progressed. Modern lamp standards, regularly spaced to give continuous high quality light can be compared here with the solitary gas lamp, offering very dim illumination over a very small distance - and this was after the war when restrictions had been lifted!

99. A view taken from 'The Spiteful', over the Welfare Ground, towards Abercarn in the late 1950s. The new-looking building to the right then housed the No.6 Area Headquarters of the National Coal Board - to which an extension had recently been added. The Prince of Wales Colliery buildings stand out with the tinworks further along.

100. The many elements of the Prince of Wales Industrial Estate have now replaced all but a small fraction of the colliery. The large white roof on the extreme left is of the tinworks main building. The top of the ex-NCB Headquarters can just be seen amongst the industrial estate buildings. It is now used by an industrial fuel-making company. The Welfare Ground has gained a more open aspect with the flattening/removal of the colliery refuse tips.

101. A well-known landmark at the entrance to Abercarn's town centre was Foxon's garage. The tinworks can be seen in the background.

102. The view again, as seen from the bottom of Rhyswg Road, displaying the A467 bypass and the roof of what was the New Tinworks (see photograph 85).

Chapter 4

Cwmcarn

103. Looking westwards at Cwmcarn, towards *'The Spiteful'*. In the left foreground was the Drill Hall, and nearer the centre, Chapel Farm. Other farms in the picture were Tir Shams yr Helwr on the extreme left, and Cilfynydd Farm high on the hillside.

104. Chapel Farm was replaced by Cwmcarn Comprehensive School, which has since become Cwmcarn High School, and the Drill Hall has been removed to make way for Priory Court, a complex of mixed dwellings. The other farms still exist, but retaining much less agricultural land - most of the hillsides in the area now bear Forestry Commission plantations.

105. An early view of Cwmcarn before many well-known streets appeared. For instance, Marne Street, (built in 1917 and named after the battle of the Marne), and the streets around the Park. Only three of the sections of Chapel Farm Terrace had been completed, the delay possibly being caused by the discovery of bones when excavating the foundations - hence the nickname *'Skeleton Row'*. Beyond was a park, later to become allotments. The Drill Hall is also missing, the dominant feature being Chapel Farm, cultivating the land later to become the Welfare Ground.

106. The missing elements referred to are now present, although from this angle so many are masked by the dense tree growth. The allotments near Chapel Farm Terrace gave way to industry. Cwmcarn High School, the Welfare Ground and parts of the Prince of Wales Industrial Estate, have collectively replaced the farm.

107. The Blair Atholl Marching Team from New Zealand, pictured outside the Drill Hall at Cwmcarn in 1952.

108. The complete team at a reunion in New Zealand in 2002 to celebrate the 50th anniversary of their tour to Britain.
From left to right, Lynn Markby, Joan O'Callaghan, Margaret Young, Gaynor Jopling, Audrey Rogers, Nylda Hoffman, Nola Rogers, Margaret Sharpe, June Adamson, Doreen Cairns, Olga McConnackie, Norma Smith, and Shirley Chapman.

Memorial Hall, Newbridge

The Blair Atholl Girls

will appear at

A LONG

DANCE

on *Friday, September, 19th.*

Music by

TERRY ALLEN
and His Dance Orchestra.

Tickets— 4/6 Single ; 8/- Double

from Members of the Entertainment Committee,
or IVOR COLLINS, The Organiser

---

109. The Blair Atholl Marching Team's tour began in March 1952, sponsored by the Rank Organisation, but, after a few months, it ran into financial difficulties.

Local charity organiser and entrepreneur, Ivor Collins, read of these problems in his newspaper, and travelled to London to meet Eric Morley. He arranged for the team to appear in the Abercarn and Cwmcarn annual carnival celebrations. Members of the team were taken in by willing families in the district, resulting in a very happy and successful week. Many lifelong friendships were formed, with letters still being exchanged between opposite ends of the world.

The programme illustrated above was actually printed in 1952 by J.R. Davies (Printers) Ltd., printers of this book.

110. A view across Chapel Farm Terrace towards Newport Road in Cwmcarn. It was obtained before 1917 as the construction of Marne Street had not begun. Nazareth Chapel stood proud. It was one of the oldest in the area, dating back to 1841. The quarry was producing building stone for the many houses being built in the area at that time.

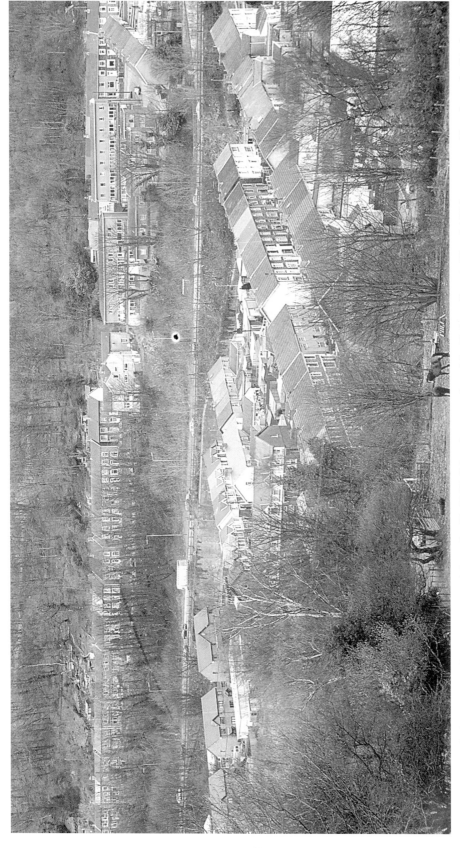

111. Not only has Marne Street appeared, but the Drill Hall has been replaced by Priory Court. The A467 bypass road has been built along the line of the canal - this section was opened in 1969. The white cottages of Chapel Row, which were opposite Nazareth Chapel, were taken down and Edwardsville built in 1970/71.

112. Looking south along the canal beside Jamesville in Cwmcarn. The White House dominated the picture, with Brierley Place behind. Rees's blacksmith's shop was just out of shot on the left.

113. The A467 bypass road now runs along the line of the old canal. Apart from some large extensions at the back of the properties in Newport Road, the residential scene is largely unaltered. The garage of New Road Motors replaced the blacksmith's.

114. Early stages in the construction of the factory for Crescent Toy Co., in 1947. The company became world famous, having an extensive export trade.

115. The factory was closed in 1982, and the premises are now utilised by Solectron Wales. Once a park, then allotments, the whole site has now been filled with industrial premises. The nearest rooftops, just seen through the trees, belong to a scrap metal business, developed along the earlier tipping site of Station Wood. High in the centre of the photograph is Tribute Avenue, developed from 1947. The A467 bypass road is seen running along the line of the filled-in canal.

116. Looking northwards along Newport Road in Cwmcarn, with the ends of the rows of Jamesville along the left-hand side. The trees in the distance were in the graveyard in front of Nazareth Chapel.

117. The newsagent's shop on the left has been a focal point in Cwmcarn for many years. It has been extended and has changed hands three times since the days of J. Miles. The corner shop at the end of Jamesville has disappeared, as has Nazareth Chapel. Next door to the newsagent's was once Briggs' footwear shop - now converted back for residential use.

118. Looking south along Newport Road, showing a glimpse of the white cottage mid-way along on the left, which stood on the site upon which Park Hall cinema was later built, (see photograph 122). On the immediate right was Cwmcarn Hotel standing at the crossroads between the main road and Jamesville/Park Street. Crossroads was the original name for Cwmcarn.

119. The hotel, now named The Cwmcarn, has gained a substantial extension with an imposing chimney. Park Hall has come and gone (1913-1972), whilst a wider road and a speedier means of transport make up the other main changes.

120. An image of Newport Road in 1950. Great use was made then of Cwmcarn Library & Institute on the right-hand side. Groups were frequently seen standing on its front steps watching the world go by, or the activities surrounding Park Hall cinema opposite.

121. The Post Office and the Institute still exist, but not so the cycle shop. Park Hall is a noticeable absentee, and a number of other shops have either closed or changed hands.

122.   The white cottage (see photograph 118), around which the adjacent terraced houses and shops were built. Behind it was a field known as The Park - later to be developed into the modern Park which was itself surrounded by residential streets.

123.   Park Hall cinema replaced the white cottage, itself being demolished in 1972, leaving part of its end wall standing. The site is now occupied by the six houses of Park Court. To the extreme right, on a piece of land that had been unoccupied for many years, stands the Cwmcarn OAP Welfare Hall.

124. Houses in John Street, Cwmcarn, were built c.1912, probably using stone quarried from the hillside behind. The picture was taken from Ivor Street, in which dwellings were constructed in 1910. In the centre was the Memorial Park - here in the early stages of development.

125. The quarry has long since ceased producing stone, and has almost disappeared beneath the ever-increasing vegetation. The cenotaph was erected in 1925.

126. Abercarn Fach, once standing in its own walled grounds between Park Street and Edward Street in Cwmcarn. It was the home of Ebenezer Rogers whilst he was manager of Abercarn Colliery, and was used in its later years as a doctor's surgery.

127. In 1953, the residential complex, also named Abercarn Fach, was established in its place. The picture here shows Park Street on the left, and Edward Street to the right of the two-storey flats. The road on the immediate left leads to Tribute Avenue.

128. The Park area of Cwmcarn in 1913, just before the opening of Park Hall cinema - seen on the extreme right. The foundations of Park Street itself were being constructed in the foreground. The space to the lower right was the later site of Tabernacle Church. Part of Caradoc Street had not been built, neither had the Infants School. Only the stables of Abercarn Fach can be made out through the trees.

129. Each missing element previously mentioned has taken its place in the scene. However, Park Hall cinema has been replaced by the houses of Park Court, and the site of Tabernacle was taken up by three houses in 1965. Between the camera position and the completed section of Park Street now stands Tribute Avenue, built in 1947.

79

130. The downcast shaft at Cwmcarn was sunk in 1876 as a ventilation aid to Prince of Wales Colliery at Abercarn. In 1912 however, the colliery began producing coal itself, and was eventually closed by the National Coal Board in 1968.

131. The colliery buildings were demolished in 1972, and an excellent restoration exercise has absorbed the colliery site into the Cwmcarn Forest Drive project. The position of the original downcast shaft is marked by a tram and a winding wheel.

132. Cwmcarn Forest Drive Visitor Centre, providing refreshments, gifts, and information on the many facilities and activities available. Down through the trees, to the left of the picture, is a car park where once stood a row of twelve houses named Millbrook Terrace.

133. The Forest Drive is seven miles long winding around the slopes of Mynydd Medart, and nearing, at its highest point, the site of an Iron Age hill fort, Twmbarlwm, (1,374ft). Other facilities include prepared routes for walking, mountain biking, and orienteering, together with a detailed programme of craft and other events. The drive has seven car parks, with many picnic and barbecue sites.

134. Nantcarn Road, c.1950. A pride was certainly taken in the upkeep of the allotments.

135. Little change in the houses themselves, and the allotments are still being fully utilised. The provision of steps, near left, eases the climb to George Street behind. The speed humps are necessary to deter through traffic from using the street as a route to Cwmcarn Forest Drive.

136. Looking back along Newport Road from a position near Cwmcarn Junior School. The white cottage is just visible and it is noticeable that there is little or no access to Ivor Street, built around 1910.

137. Several changes to commercial premises are in evidence, but the houses on the far right remain largely unaltered. Ivor Street now runs off to the right towards the park.

138. Meat was certainly one of the priorities on the shopping list in those days. This was one of several butcher's shops in the district. Sayce's later moved further along Newport Road. Behind the shop on the left can be seen the British Legion hall.

139. A wider fare on offer now at the Spar minimarket. The British Legion hall has been converted into Cwmcarn Boxing Club, now used by Joe Calzaghe following the demolition of the Newbridge gymnasium, (see photograph 55).

Chapter 5

Pontywaun

140. Leisurely times in Twyncarn Road in Pontywaun and a gardener's delight! The road turned to the right over Pontywaun Bridge and towards Crosskeys.

141. A row of cottages on the left has given way to a children's play area, and the gardeners have obviously cleaned up!

142. A very old image of Factory Trip, the hill linking Cwmcarn and Pontywaun. Twyncarn House commanded the landscape, with the canal being a strong and important feature.

143. A funeral procession negotiating Factory Trip in 1924. Additional buildings are now seen on the left-hand side of the hill. Staite's Billiard Hall stands alongside the road, and behind it can be seen the ruins of a club which was burned down on Boxing Night 1923.

The Monmouthshire, Brecon and Abergavenny Canals Trust.

Since this book was published more information about the Monmouthshire, Brecon and Abergavenny Canal has been passed to the authors. In 2001, the Trust invested £3,000 with an additional £3,000 from Caerphilly County Borough Council and volunteers built a slipway for boats into the canal at Halls Road. This followed two years of work by Trust volunteers to open the section from Pontywaun to the Darren for boating activities. The Trust is an active member of the Monmouthshire Canal Restoration Scheme.

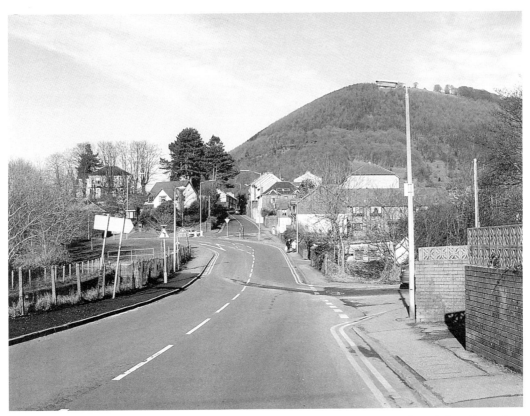

144. The valley towns have now been bypassed by the new A467 road, and the old road can be seen to veer off to the left towards the nearby junction.

The billiards hall is no more, and Twyncarn House, now a Day Centre, is becoming heavily screened by the trees.

The right turn just ahead of the camera position is the access road to Cwmcarn Forest Drive. It was formed along the route of the branch railway line which served Cwmcarn Colliery.

From a point near the left turn sign the canal has been filled in as far as Chapel of Ease to accommodate the building of the new road, although it still survives southwards to link up with the Brecon & Abergavenny Canal. This, the Crumlin Branch of the Monmouthshire Canal, was completed in 1799. It was 11 miles long, containing 32 locks, and its commercial use ended in 1930. For many years since, the canal has been, and still is in parts, in a poor condition, overgrown and polluted both by the public and by industry. Various attempts have been made to improve this situation, but the good work has been negated by lack of funding amongst other things. More recently, however, very much to the credit of the Islwyn Canal Association, and of Caerphilly County Borough Council, a great deal of work has been carried out. By the summer of 2003 a 1,300m stretch from Manor Road to Henry Roberts Bridge in Risca had undergone a major renovation. This had entailed upgrading of the towpath, relining of a section, dredging and reshaping the remaning length, together with extensive tree surgery. This section now forms part of the National Cycle Network.

It is to be hoped that, this renovation work being completed, regular maintenance will ensure that the canal remains a valuable asset to the district.

145. The Flannel Factory at Pontywaun which was flooded on 18th July 1875. The disaster resulted in the deaths of the owner John Hunt, his wife and four children, together with two servants and an apprentice. It was caused by the bursting of a dam containing the feeder reservoir. North Road and Coronation Place create the background.

146. The site of the factory is now a little overgrown, and is contained between the old and new roads, with a roundabout leading into nearby Pontywaun. There has been quite a lot of housing development over the years, and the railway leading to Cwmcarn Colliery was replaced by the access road to Cwmcarn Forest Drive - the entry is seen on the extreme right of the picture. The tall building near the centre was, from 1971, Kingdom Hall of the Risca Congregation of Jehovah's Witnesses, but it has recently been sold for conversion into flats.

147. Old and new Hall's Bridges, which were part of Hall's Tramroad, built by Benjamin Hall. His son's name, also Benjamin, is linked to the famous bell in the clock tower at Westminster. He was a Member of Parliament, and the bell was cast whilst he was Commissioner for Works.

The bridges enabled rolling stock to cross over from the western side to the eastern side of the valley at Pontywaun. The replacement bridge, built in 1853, became necessary due to increasing wheel base for rail traffic as opposed to trams, so that larger radius curves were required at its ends. Steam engines had by then replaced horses, which had been banned from the tramroads in 1849.

Hall's Tramroad, completed in 1811, ran from Crosskeys, via a tunnel at Pentwynmawr, to Waterloo Colliery, later to become part of Oakdale Colliery.

At much the same time, the Sirhowy Tramroad, running from Tredegar to Newport along the Sirhowy Valley, was completed, crossing the Ebbw Valley at Risca. It was not until 1827, however, that a tramroad was constructed to complete the link between Risca and Crosskeys.

Hall's Tramroad was taken over by the Great Western Railway in 1876, and the section running alongside Cwmcarn and Abercarn was locally referred to as *'the top line'*. *'The bottom line'*, being the Western Valley Line, had been opened to passenger traffic from Newport to Blaina in 1850. The speed limit was 10 mph. What's changed? An arch of the original stone bridge still exists over the river.

148. A different elevation which shows the steel frame piers of the newer bridge. These were to be changed again due to increasing freight loads - see below.

149. The *'new'* bridge, with its original piers changed to masonry, remained in use for many years to serve Oakdale Colliery. Its main purpose now seems to be as a magnet for graffiti artists.

Chapter 6

Crosskeys

150. The view down High Street in Crosskeys from a position near the Eagle Inn towards *'Crosskeys Co-op'*. The footbridge on the left crossed the line of Hall's Tramroad to gain access to Hall's Road. An active roadsweeper - perhaps for the benefit of the cameraman!

151. The Eagle Inn is now simply called The Eagle. The two shops on the right have been lost, and the *'Co-op'* has changed its function (see photograph 157). The footbridge now crosses an overgrown disused line.

152. Carlton Terrace, Crosskeys, around 1910. The railway station is clearly seen in the background, and the subway at the bottom of the hill to the right led to Crosskeys Corner.

153. Very little about Carlton Terrace has changed, and the road has hardly altered as it disappears beneath the subway. The main absentee here is the station, although the track still runs along its original route. Plans are afoot at the time of publication to reopen the line and to replace the station.

154. Looking northwards along High Street, Crosskeys, c.1910. On the immediate right is Hope Baptist Church, built in 1880. Next to it is the building erected by Risca and Crosskeys Co-operative Society.

155. Hope chapel is still active, but the building next door has been put to alternative uses - the first floor area is taken up by the Red Triangle Snooker Club. The smaller shops have been lost, but otherwise the scene has changed very little.

156. The Risca and Crosskeys Co-operative Society building later belonged to Blaina Industrial and Provident Society, and was commonly known as *'Crosskeys Co-op'*.

157. Various businesses have made use of the lower floor, and the upper floor has been, since 1982, utilised by the Red Triangle Snooker Club, recently acquired by the local professional player, Darren Morgan.

158. The view back up High Street, Crosskeys, from above the subway. Quite a gathering outside Hope chapel - probably congregating for the Whitsun march. Crosskeys Hotel is on the left of the picture.

159. The lower access to the hotel, now named The Cross Keys, has been removed and the road widened with the provision of a bus stop. Hope chapel can just be seen through the trees. The photograph was taken from the old station approach, which may well be in use again quite soon with the proposed reopening of the railway line.

160. A ton of coal waiting to be carried through someone's house in Gladstone Street. Crosskeys Miners' Institute, on the immediate right, was constructed in 1911 out of lodge funds. It boasted one of the most up-to-date libraries in the area.

161. The Institute was replaced by the flats of Ebbw Court in the late 1980s. St. Catherine's Church is mostly hidden behind the trees, and some of the houses in the terrace block to the left have been converted into shops. Just imagine the traffic chaos that load of coal would cause today!

162. Penniless Corner, Crosskeys, a gathering point for the unemployed - pictured here in the 1920s.

163. A wider view showing the alterations that have been made around Penniless Corner. The old A467, renamed the B4591, still runs under the railway bridge towards Pontywaun, with the new A467 bypass, completed in 1976, being accessed via the link road shown. The Miners' Institute has been replaced by blocks of flats, just seen on the extreme left of the picture.

164. The Primitive Methodist Church, on Gladstone Street Crosskeys, was built in 1879. Beyond it can be seen the entrance to St. Catherine's Church, and then Crosskeys Miners' Institute. In the far distance was the station approach and footbridge in front of Carlton Terrace.

165. Conversion of the Primitive Methodist Church into a car park exposes St. Catherine's to view. Hidden here by the trees, the Miners' Institute has been replaced by the flats of Ebbw Court.

166. Looking in the other direction, we see that the street beyond the Primitive Methodist Church was yet to be developed.

167. The missing houses are now seen beyond the car park, and it is interesting to note that the dwelling house on the immediate left of the picture has been converted into a shop - the reverse of the general trend.

168. Moving further along, Gladstone Street is seen in its commercial heyday, sporting more than forty shops.

169. Just a few of those shops now remain, the others being converted into dwelling houses, and the inevitable traffic-calming feature has been added.

170. A view looking southwards from Crosskeys Corner along Risca Road. The attractive cottages in the foreground formed Woodland Place.

171. The cottages have long since lost their front gardens and become shops. Just after the Second World War, Joe's Café gained a wide reputation for delicious ice cream. The first property in the next block has changed in use from a fish shop whilst the second still houses Crosskeys Post Office.

172. Waunfawr Primary School, which opened in 1897. It was burned down in 1905 and later rebuilt. This picture was taken before Waunfawr Road was constructed, the school then looking out over a field.

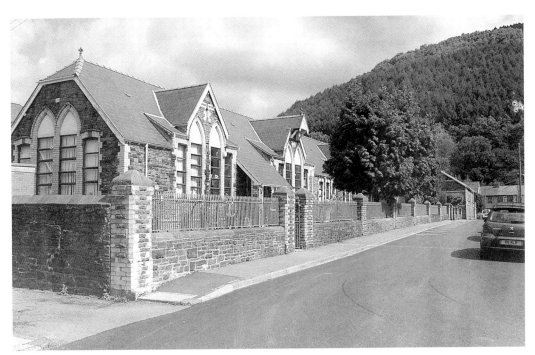

173. Waunfawr Road has appeared but the profile of the school remains very much the same.

174. A view of Crosskeys before many well-known landmarks were added. Crosskeys College had not been built, neither had the Western Welsh bus garage. Blackvein Colliery and the Sirhowy Tramroad can be seen, as can the road leading across from Blackvein. Houses on Waunfawr Park Road, built in 1927, are seen middle right, and some structures on the main road in the foreground are recognisable.

175. The college now forms the Crosskeys Campus of Coleg Gwent. It opened in 1961 as The Technical College of Monmouthshire, being moved from its earlier location at Crumlin, (see photograph 17). In 1974 it was changed to a College of Further Education, and in 1976 became a Tertiary College. The Western Welsh garage has come and gone, and the line of the Sirhowy Tramroad is now taken up by the bypass road. Blackvein Road can still be seen, and the houses of Waunfawr Gardens, to the left, complete the picture.

176. An elevated view of Crosskeys, looking northwards, taken in the early 1960s - soon after the college was opened. Before the days of the bypass, the main road ran amongst the buildings and in front of the college - seen to the right. A clear feature is the railway line, right in the centre, which was still in great demand for freight, mainly by the collieries.

177. A few buildings have been added by the college, and the flats replacing the Institute are seen centre left. The most important addition is the bypass road, seen to the left as it rounds Pandy Park, home of Crosskeys Rugby Football Club. The railway line which served Cwmcarn and Oakdale Collieries is now overgrown, but the '*bottom line*', which runs on up the Western Valley, is seen crossing the bypass to the left. This picture attracts the eye northwards, over Abercarn, as far as Treowen which overlooks Newbridge.

107

178. The Round House, Crosskeys. Originally constructed as a Toll House under the Abercarn Turnpike Roads Trust Commissioners, possibly to levy a charge upon the coal coming from the Blackvein Colliery on its way to the canal.

Medart Place stands opposite, and the presence of the uniformed policeman gives some clue as to the age of the picture.

179. Various changes and extensions to the Round House have noticeably increased its size, but the overall shape has been retained. The two houses filling the gap in Medart Place were built in 1906.

180. A picture of Medart Place taken in the opposite direction, (looking to the south), shows the road, which now passes along Cromwell Road, appearing to turn to the left - perhaps being the shortest route to the canal.

181. Medart Place has hardly changed, but Cromwell Road has appeared in the distance.

Chapter 7

Risca & Pontymister

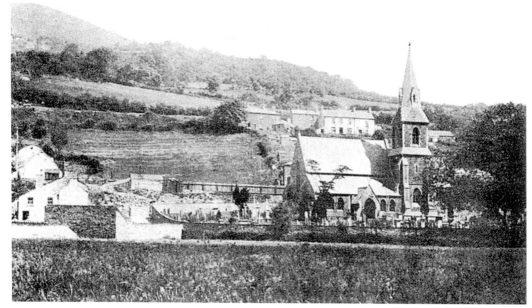

182. St. Mary's Church was opened in 1853, although other churches previously existed on the site. These possibly dated back to the 13th century or even earlier. This picture was taken before the Sunday School was built in the field in the foreground in 1891.

183. The camera angle has been turned slightly to show the amount of development around and behind the church, especially up towards Fernlea. Holly Road, to the right, rises up to the Ty Sign development.

184. Risca Urban District Council was formed under the Local Government Act in 1894, and was disbanded in 1974 upon the formation of Islwyn Borough Council.

185. The old Urban District Council Office is now utilised by Risca Male Choir as their Headquarters and Rehearsal Room. To the left is Risca Day Hospital.

186. Long Bridge, Risca, which carried the Sirhowy Tramroad across from one side of the valley to the other. It was 40 to 50 feet high, and contained 33 arches. Being built for trams it was unsuitable for rail traffic and was bypassed in 1853, then finally demolished at the end of the 19th century. The stone recovered was used in the building of Bridge Street. The brickworks can be seen to the left, with Tir-y-Cwm Farm in the foreground.

187. Remains of the eastern abutment of the bridge can be found in the side of the B4591 road, near the junction between Grove Road and St. Mary Street - close to the building with the bright white roof to the right of the picture. The open space between the bridge and Dan-y-Graig Road is now taken up by houses, including those off Clarence Place and Phillip Street. The bypass road, seen in the left foreground, follows the line of the tramroad from Crosskeys to the starting point of the old bridge. It then bypasses Risca, Pontymister and Rogerstone before joining with Forge Lane in Bassaleg prior to the junction with the M4 motorway. The farmhouse still exists to the left of the bypass.

188. Glyn Congregational Church, Risca, on the junction of Tredegar Street and Dan-y-Graig Road. It was built in 1858 and demolished in 1990.

189. Following the removal of the Glyn Chapel, Dan-y-Graig Church was built. In 2000, a building extension was added to form a local ecumenical partnership of Methodist, Presbyterian and United Reform Churches.

190. Moriah Chapel, on Tredegar Street in Risca, was built in 1893, replacing *'Old Moriah'* on the same site.

191. Road widening has taken place and the inevitable provision made for car parking. Despite the bypass road, Risca and Pontymister have remained busy commercial areas with many more shops thriving than in most other valley towns.

192. Tredegar Grounds, commonly known as Risca Park. The facility was donated to to the town and opened by Lord Tredegar in 1902.

193. The park has been retained as an attractive open space for the people of Risca, even though the town has seen a great deal of development over the years. The schoolroom extension was added to Moriah Chapel in September 1995. Glyn Chapel, just seen in the top of the photograph opposite Moriah, was demolished in 1990.

194. Tredegar Street, Risca, c.1910. Vandalism was unheard of at that time as the ornate lamps on the milliner's shop testify. Great foresight would seem to have been shown in the width to which both the road and the pavement were constructed. The roof of Glyn Chapel can be seen rising above all the others.

195. The benefits arising out of the widths of the road and the pavement now become clear. The footpath is still substantial, but space has been made for vehicle parking along the whole length of the street and the roadway is sufficiently wide for some waiting on the opposite side. During the working day, parking is still at a premium, indicating the popularity of the area despite the nearby provision of supermarkets.

196. The canal bridge on Moriah Hill in Risca, being negotiated by a horse-drawn barge.

197. A great deal of renovation work has been already carried out on this part of the canal with more being promised.

198. Bethany Baptist Chapel, Pontymister, was built in 1858 and rebuilt in 1875.

199. The chapel itself has remained relatively unchanged - not so its surroundings. Pontymister school, to the left, has been demolished, and Lidl's supermarket built. These changes give a much clearer view of Risca Rugby Football Club, which includes a Sports and Fitness Centre.

200. Commercial Street, Pontymister, c.1910. St. Margaret's Church is seen on the right-hand side, and Bethany Chapel ahead on the left.

201. The shop frontages, as further along in Tredegar Street, Risca, now include vehicle parking spaces - empty above as the photograph was taken on a Sunday morning. The addition of the footpath on the right-hand side still leaves a relatively wide roadway. Just beyond Bethany Chapel is the Risca Palace cinema which has been empty for some time, although repair and re-use is soon to take place.

202. Commercial Street, Pontymister, displaying a very slow pace of life, around 1910. Again, the road width for this form of transport was surprising. Pontywaun County School, midway along on the right, would have been comparatively new.

203. Plenty of room for parking on both sides of the street. Rather more shops on the left - a reverse of the general trend. The Brooklands Training Centre, replacing the County School, (see photograph 204), is behind the tall tree on the right.

204. Pontywaun County School. Its beginnings were in temporary accommodation at Crosskeys in 1898. The foundation stone for the new building at Pontymister was laid by Lord Tredegar in 1899, with the opening ceremony taking place in November 1900. The title later became Pontywaun County Grammar School, and it was closed in 1963.

205. The site of the school is now occupied by Brooklands Social Services Adult Training Centre. The original stone wall, pillars and entrance gate are still standing.

206. Floodwaters spilled over from the River Ebbw in 1979 with devastating effect in Commercial Street, Pontymister.

207. A drier scene with a few changes made to the affected properties. The flood prevention work carried out on the banks of the river has proved to be successful, with no major problems since.

208. The Rolling Mill Hotel, Pontymister, in the 1920s. Its location was near Pontymister Crossing which carried a rail link to the steelworks. The Leyland bus, operated by the Western Valley Omnibus Services, sets the scene.

209. The name is now simply The Rolling Mill, and the advance of time is seen in the need to provide entertainment in the modern public house - both in the live form and by way of satellite television. At least the bus-stop has remained at the same place!

210. Pontymister Steelworks in its smoky prime. Its history dates back to the early 1800s, when the site contained an ironworks. Tin-plate production started in 1843, and by the end of the century, steel had become the focus.

211. The steelworks closed upon the rationalisation of steel-making at Llanwern, being replaced by Pontymister Industrial Estate, with units varying in size and in nature of usage. This photograph, taken from Mill Street, captures several properties on the far hillside, including those at Och-y-Wyth, which are still standing. They certainly are benefiting from the reduced amount of smoke in the atmosphere.

212. This bridge carried, until recent years, the access road to the hamlet of Och-y-Wyth high on the hillside overlooking Pontymister.

213. The route to Och-y-Wyth was truncated by the bypass road - vehicles can just be made out through the trees. A new access road was constructed from a roundabout junction a little further north. The old stone bridge now only serves as a farm access.

214./215. In this book it has not been the intention to deal in depth with the history of the area, but to supply background information to make comparison of the old and new photographs meaningful. There are several excellent local history books to which the reader is referred. In addition, it is strongly recommended that a visit be paid to the Industrial History Museum at Oxford House Community Education Centre in Risca.

The Oxford House Industrial Archaeology Society (later renamed Oxford House Industrial History Society) was founded in 1971, and first put together the museum at Pontymister School in 1977. For several reasons new premises were sought, and in 1996, Islwyn Borough Council acquired the Risca Collieries Workmen's Institute on behalf of Oxford House. Being next door to the Centre, it provides the ideal home for the numerous exhibits, which as the picture shows, includes photographs, charts, historical accounts, etc., spread throughout a number of rooms.